THE
SPIRIT
RECOVERY
MEDITATION JOURNAL

THE SPIRIT RECOVERY MEDITATION JOURNAL

Meditations for Reclaiming Your Authenticity

Lee McCormick

Health Communications, Inc.
Deerfield Beach, Florida

www.hcibooks.com

Library of Congress Cataloging-in-Publication Data
is availabe from the Library of Congress.

Publisher: Health Communications, Inc.
         3201 S.W. 15th Street
         Deerfield Beach, FL 33442-8190

Spirit Recovery logo by Ted Raess at Raess Design
Cover and Inside design by Larissa Hise Henoch
Inside book formatting by Dawn Von Strolley Grove

The Twelve Steps of Alcoholics Anonymous

1. We admitted we were powerless over alcohol—that our lives had become unmanageable.
2. Came to believe that a Power greater than ourselves could restore us to sanity.
3. Made a decision to turn our will and our lives over to the care of God as we understood Him.
4. Made a searching and fearless moral inventory of ourselves.
5. Admitted to God, to ourselves, and to another human being the exact nature of our wrongs.
6. Were entirely ready to have God remove all these defects of character.
7. Humbly asked Him to remove our shortcomings.
8. Made a list of all persons we had harmed, and became willing to make amends to them all.
9. Made direct amends to such people wherever possible, except when to do so would injure them or others.
10. Continued to take personal inventory and when we were wrong promptly admitted it.
11. Sought through prayer and meditation to improve our conscious contact with God, as we understood Him, praying only for knowledge of His will for us and the power to carry that out.
12. Having had a spiritual awakening as the result of these Steps, we tried to carry this message to alcoholics, and to practice these principles in all our affairs.

With all my love and gratitude to Benjamin Richard McCormick, Pauline Kirk Davis, Aretimus Darius Davis, Idora McCullough, Barbara Lynn McCormick, Benjamin Bachlour McCormick, Dean and Julie Norton, Sue Bissel, David Osinga, Michael Brown, Lynde Stich, Albert Sombrero, Miguel Rivera, Gary Siedler and my editor, James Morris. To my daughters, Alexis McCormick Kirby, Anastasia Marie McCormick, and Isabella Lee McCormick, and my granddaughter, Sydney Elizabeth Kirby. To my best friend and esposa, Mee Tracy McCormick, and to all of those who have touched The Ranch. A special thanks to my friends and teachers Ted and Peggy Raess and to Barbara Emrys and Don Miguel Ruiz for the minimal chance. This book is dedicated to the journey—may we have the eyes to see and the ears to hear.

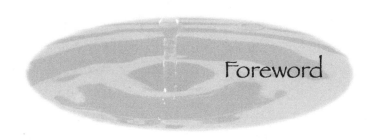

Foreword

This beautiful book is an expression of the desire to transform our lives. We live in a society that supports the addiction to suffering. For thousands of years, people have believed that they came into this world to suffer. This belief is preached by religions and many other philosophies. Our investment in such a belief makes it appear true.

As children growing up, we receive a lot of information that distorts the truth of who we are. The adults in our lives teach us what to believe about belonging, being loved and feeling safe. We learn to alter our behavior in order to fit in, which results in the loss of our authenticity.

Believing that we are not the way that we should be according to the rules of society leads to self-rejection. To recover from a lifetime of such conditioning, we must become aware. Awareness is the minimal chance for change. In increasing our awareness, we begin to experience ourselves as we are, not the way we were taught we should be and continue to pretend to be. People who do not reject themselves do not perceive rejection. People who see and accept life as it is do not perceive life through suffering.

The daily meditations in this book were written by Lee McCormick, a wonderful human being who has recovered from his own ideas of suffering. Lee has worked as my apprentice for several years. His personal experiences will inspire you to deepen your self-awareness, and with each daily passage, he offers you a chance to recover the connection with your authenticity.

I have a lot of gratitude for the courage in every individual to face the truth, to uncover the false beliefs that have been ruling his or her life, and to make changes. By shifting ourselves, humanity shifts also, and suffering transforms into constant gratitude for life itself. This book is a beautiful contribution to that evolution.

All my love and blessings,
Don Miguel Angel Ruiz

Don Miguel Ruiz is the author of *The Four Agreements,* a *New York Times* bestseller, *The Mastery of Love, The Four Agreements Companion Book, Prayers* and *The Voice of Knowledge.*

Introduction

Spirit Recovery is the recovery of our integrity, the process of reclaiming truth from all the distortions and lies that ruin our lives.

Out of my personal process the concept of Spirit Recovery was born. This book is a sharing of the evolution of my awareness, that awareness without which we cannot recover. These meditations were written through me, for me. From one point of view they are very personal, and from another they are not personal at all.

In 1997 life took me to a place where every aspect of who and what I believed I was became subject to question. As resistance to change arose, and my insistence that I knew who I was was challenged, I realized that I didn't really believe the me I was defending.

My journey into recovery quickly became about a lot more than the addictions and behaviors that got me admitted to a treatment center. Recovery became a doorway back to truth and life.

As I moved through the process, it became obvious that I was being offered a new program for life, the life of a recovering person. I was not interested in trying to fit into another new program. What I wanted was freedom.

To be more specific, I wanted the "happy, joyous and free" that Bill W. talked about in the *Big Book* of AA. I wanted to recover from all that I had tried to be and reclaim who I really was.

Over the next eight years I practiced being a student of life, involving myself in every experience or teaching that hooked my attention. I came to realize that what I had considered a comfort zone was not comfortable at all. It was only familiar. The pathway to freedom required an unraveling of the beliefs, agreements, behaviors and secrets that held together my image of myself.

The power this book holds is its ability to provoke a questioning of perception and belief. As an adult I am completely responsible for how I see life and what I choose to believe about life.

The Spirit Recovery Meditation Journal is meant to be read in the spirit of AA's "90 meetings in 90 days." The intention of each meditation is to help you clear your mind and allow you to express yourself through the journaling process. When you arise in the morning, take a moment to read a meditation. As you read the meditations allow all the thoughts and feelings that surface for you to flow onto the journal pages. Don't think; just write one word after another, without judgment. My only suggestion in using this book is that you work through it with absolute commitment to yourself and with ruthless honesty.

There is a power offered to us when we are willing to show

up for ourselves. It is the power of grace, and miracles occur in the presence of grace. So go for it; keep showing up. Life does work if you work it.

Thank you for reading this book, and thank you for taking responsibility for life. Together we are doing the work of the angels, transforming our legacies from fear and suffering to love and opportunity. We are worthy, and we are worth it.

Peace be with you.

Sincerely,
Lee McCormick

MEDITATIONS

Who Am I?

If I am not the person I have believed myself to be, then who am I? Actually, I'm grateful to hear that maybe I'm not the anti-Christ. That is a relief, but who am I? I have lived for so long with all the stories and behaviors of my disease that I've lost my connection to whoever is underneath that.

That's who I'm looking for in recovery, who I really am. I have tried for so long to be who or what I thought people wanted or told me to be that I don't want to do that again. I don't want to be defined by the world around me. To not be sure of who I think I am is really scary. In fact my question of identity leaves me hanging out over a deep black void. "Keep coming back;" those are the gentle words of support whispered in my ear.

This journey is not easy. To have strayed so far from my truth is sad, but it's all going to work out if I keep showing up for myself. Today I will stay committed to living happy, joyous and free. That is the gift that recovery has offered, and that is where I am headed.

I'm Not Bad—I've Just Been Crazy

I don't know exactly how it happened. What I do know is that, as I've realized how grateful I am for my recovery, I have also realized that I love myself and my life. It must be a package deal, like one of those all-inclusive resorts. Gratitude opened the door to the truth, which allowed me to see myself through my own eyes of gratitude.

I'm not bad—I've just been crazy. Seeing myself with gratitude allowed me to see the beauty in my life, which reflected my own image back to me. I am the perceiver. I am the projector. When I didn't like myself, how could I like anyone else?

Sometimes I am amazed at how easily I have misled myself. I have believed so many ridiculous things, most of which I used against myself. Things like, I am not good enough, or not talented enough or whatever.

All of that served to support what I had chosen to believe about myself. I created the stories that would support my beliefs. It was all me, all along.

I don't do that anymore. Today I look out at life and see myself reflected back in the smiles of the people around me. There is no need for a story. When I chose to like myself I chose to stop believing my own lies about myself, and that changed everything. Recovery is a matter of choices, and today I choose life.

_____

_____

_____

_____

_____

_____

_____

_____

_____

_____

_____

_____

_____

_____

_____

_____

_____

_____

_____

_____

I Didn't See It Coming

I didn't see it coming.

The voice of judgment is screaming that I am a failure, an incurable addict and a loser. I want to indulge myself in that old, repulsive self-hatred.

I used. Call it a slip, a relapse, a whatever. The truth is I did what I have done for years, despite all the work I've done on myself.

Now is when I have a choice to practice the compassion and acceptance that gets so much lip service in the recovery world. To be in judgment of myself or allow others to judge me, is pure poison, and that is the last thing I need.

Courage asks, what can I learn from this experience? What is the truth about what I have done? No excuses. No judgment.

If I learn from the experience, then I have benefited from it.

Keep it simple. No one else can interpret this situation for me. That is my responsibility. I can ask for help but not the judgment of others.

This is the real deal. We can tell the truth of how far we've really come when the devil's back in town. I will be gentle with myself today. I'll be careful not to gossip about myself. I know I have come a long way, and I will not throw that away.

Keep coming back. That's the key. Keep showing up. Recovery is a process, not a scorecard.

_____

_____

_____

_____

_____

_____

_____

_____

_____

_____

_____

_____

_____

_____

_____

_____

_____

_____

_____

_____

The Moon Was Full Last Night

I stood outside, looking up, and experienced déjà vu of when I was fifteen. I could feel the feelings and wonder I had felt then.

The experience was powerful. In that moment, being where I am today and feeling another place in time, I realized that within my being I not only carry the memories of pain and fear, I also carry the memories of joy and wonder.

It was so cool to realize that.

Yes, there *was* a time in my life before everything got crazy. Life was an adventure, and I was the lead character in that adventure. What I realize this morning is that, as I unravel the life I've lived, I'm going to find a lot of sweet, happy memories along with the painful, scary ones. Life is not all or nothing.

The truth is that somewhere along the way I lost my connection to the happy me and fell into a pattern of suffering and struggling. Belief follows attention. If our physical bodies are what we eat, literally, then our emotional selves become what we eat emotionally.

I have eaten a lot of misery, misery that I cooked up.

It feels good to see how I have been responsible for creating my own suffering. Knowing that gives me the power to say, "No more." I am learning how I live in this world; the journey of recovery offers me back my life.

Today I will look for the gifts of awareness and be grateful for them all, one day at a time.

_____

_____

_____

_____

_____

_____

_____

_____

_____

_____

_____

_____

_____

_____

_____

_____

_____

_____

_____

Flying Dreams

I dreamed last night that I could fly. I've had those flying dreams all my life, and they are still an amazing sensation. Most of the time, I am fleeing something or someone. I have spent a lot of time running from life. Out of that need to run I developed so many crazy behaviors and beliefs.

Today I no longer need to run. I can count on me today. I have choices that support working through my fears. I no longer have to live in reaction. I no longer have to believe what I think. That's the power of recovering my truth. Today I will trust my instincts. I will walk into life with my eyes and heart open to the truth, my truth. Today I will love my life unconditionally. Breathe, feel, live, love.

_____

_____

_____

_____

_____

_____

_____

_____

_____

_____

_____

_____

_____

_____

_____

_____

_____

_____

_____

Just a Little Lazy

Today I am slow waking up. I remember all those mornings when waking up was misery. Today I am just a little lazy, and you know . . . so what? I feel my body. I feel the dreamtime, like a blanket wrapped around me.

I love feeling my being today. Whether I'm Mr. Slow Motion or ready to take on the world, I like being me, and that is loving life on life's terms.

Today I will take it easy and see what moving a little slower has to reveal to me.

This is my life. Thank you, Creator, I love you. One day at a time.

_____

_____

_____

_____

_____

_____

_____

_____

_____

_____

_____

_____

_____

_____

_____

_____

_____

_____

I Didn't Get My Way

Yesterday I was in one of those situations that really irritates me. I wanted my way, and that didn't happen, so I was pissed. I even woke up in the middle of the night and ran the event through my head over and over. I am still crazy.

As I become aware of how ingrained my reactions and programming are, I am amazed at how persistent my way of thinking can be. Recovery is truly a remarkable experience. I am re-creating how I interact with life and the world. This is about so much more than the addictions and behaviors that got me here. Today I am going to appreciate me for showing up for myself. Loving myself begins with simple appreciation and gratitude for myself.

I am changing who I am, and I am looking forward to life one day at a time.

Seven Meetings in Seven Days

Today I make the commitment to myself that I will go to seven 12-step meetings in the next seven days.

I'll do my best to just listen, unless I am in crisis. I'll take a journal with me, and I'll write my feelings after the meeting. I make this commitment to show up for myself and to practice being present, observing without having to say anything. I will listen, not allowing reaction to go beyond my mind chatter. I will exercise my will over the need to speak out or react. By learning to observe life without reaction I am becoming the master of my life and relinquishing the victim's role.

I See a Museum of
Personal Ancient History

I am going to have a giveaway garage sale.

Looking around my home, I see a museum of personal ancient history. This stuff is not me anymore. I actually don't know that this stuff ever was me. Who cares? I'm not dragging all this junk around anymore.

How crazy is it that I've been living with a sentimental attachment to bullshit? I've got to laugh at myself. The whole time I've been working on freeing myself from suffering, I've been maintaining a museum of personal drama.

I'm crazy! How can I judge myself when it's obvious that I'm not sane enough to stand trial?

Cleaning house applies on many levels. So, let's get on with it. This is a new interpretation of "Let go and let God."

As I rearrange my life, I am also going to re-create the space I live in. Let's have a little light and fresh air here. Recovery is a reckoning with the past and an embracing of the future by becoming fully present.

As I let go of my old stuff, there will be feelings and a few tears. By letting go, I am making space for the life I live today.

Thank you, Creator, for my awakening. I love you.

They Call It the First Step

"We admitted we were powerless and that our lives had become unmanageable." They call it the first step. I say "they" because I've still not acknowledged those in recovery as my people. I still feel alone. The rooms of the 12-step programs are a big part of my support system, but there is much more to my life than my relationship with the program.

I am powerless over my addictions when I indulge them. That is absolutely true. The rest of the truth is that I am not powerless in my ability to make a choice other than indulging in my addictions. If I were powerless over my ability to choose I would not be here now. Accepting the truth of my situation is empowering. Acknowledging the unmanageability of my using is simply being honest.

My own self-judgment kept me from the gifts of accepting the truth of the first step. I do not believe the voice of that judge any longer. I will also not see myself as less-than because I can't successfully manage an addiction that is stupid in the first place. The power of choice is there for those willing to accept it.

I want to be free, and I won't let the chatter in my mind stand in the way of my seeking that freedom. I admitted I was powerless and my life had become unmanageable.

Today my powerlessness is in my past, and I am doing my best to keep it that way.

The Phone Was Like a Witness

The phone rang. As I turned to answer it, I realized that there was no anxiety or fear about who might be on the other end.

For a long time the phone was like a witness to my life. Using would begin with phone calls. After a run, I would hide in my house, dreading the phone ringing. I didn't want to be connected to the world. I wanted to hide. The phone would remind me of all that I had withdrawn from in my misery.

None of that is true today. I am not afraid of the telephone. I am not hiding. I don't always answer it, but that's not out of guilt or fear. There are times I am so at peace and content that I don't want to be distracted by the outside world. Talk about progress. Today I am realizing that my life is growing and changing in many wonderful ways. Today I will look at myself in the mirror and acknowledge how far I've come on this path to freedom.

My First Reaction
Was a Fearful Skepticism

A couple days ago a friend invited me to a Native American sweat lodge ceremony. I'd heard of the sweat lodge but knew little about it. My first reaction was a fearful skepticism. Then a voice of willingness whispered, "Why not?" I said yes, and that was that.

The experience was incredible.

Recovery offers so many new opportunities. I love this way of life. As I grow, the chances to participate in life grow. I can see now how much of my old behavior was a reaction to how frustrating and small my life seemed to be. Recovery is my opportunity to live the beauty and grace that embracing life offers. Freedom lies beyond my comfort zone. My attachment to comfort was, in truth, fear, and fear is not what I choose for myself today.

Today I will embrace the opportunities to live, learn and grow.

Progress, Not Perfection

I had no idea how many feelings I would have once I stopped medicating them. Amazing!

The next step is to stay present with all these feelings and not live in constant reaction to them. This is going to take some practice. Progress, not perfection. I guess after years of ignoring, stuffing and medicating my emotions I could expect the dam of emotional energy to be holding back a lot of old, heavy stuff. Easy does it. What is important now is that I don't judge myself over this emotional unraveling. The judgments would be poison, and it's poison I'm getting rid of.

I have made a commitment to myself to be gentle and thorough, to take responsibility for my reactions, and not use anything as an excuse to go against myself by going back to my old ways.

I may need to tear this page out and read it ten times a day for a while, and that's okay, too. This work of recovery is truly an art form. I am creating a new way of living in this world, one day at a time.

I Know Nothing About It

A friend has invited me to attend a study group on *A Course in Miracles*. I know nothing about it. This is a great opportunity for me to witness how closed-minded I am.

Being in recovery has put me face-to-face with the truth of my willingness or unwillingness to be open-minded. If I am not growing, I am going backward.

Life moves forward, expanding, feeding on the objects of my attention. To grow spiritually can only happen beyond the limitations of judgments and fears.

I'm going to go to this class that I know nothing about. Bill W. says, matter-of-factly, in the *Big Book*, that AA is a spiritual program. Spirituality is life, and life has offered me the chance to participate in my own growth. I do know that I want and need more from recovery than not using and going to meetings.

As I heal I look forward to opportunities to push myself. I don't know much about living happy, joyous and free, but I have every intention of getting there.

_____

_____

_____

_____

_____

_____

_____

_____

_____

_____

_____

_____

_____

_____

_____

_____

_____

_____

_____

_____

_____

I Need to Get Real Simple

Sometimes I'm overwhelmed with it all.

I've been doing everything right, and I still feel lost and overwhelmed. This is when I need to get real simple. Next week, tomorrow, today even, is too much.

When I'm in my overwhelmed place, my focus comes down to the moment. In the moment, I can check in on the truth of where I'm at. I feel sad, depressed, and there is no obvious reason why. It's just how I feel.

So, okay!

I don't need to judge myself or even have an opinion on what's going on with me. I can shift my attention to the positive in my life and, while still honoring my feelings, choose to be grateful for growth and progress.

By taking responsibility for my attention, I reclaim the power to choose. I am not a victim unless I choose to be a victim; that is my choice, my responsibility. Today I will keep it simple, feeling my feelings and choosing the focus of my attention.

Compassion begins with myself. I will love myself, and my life, in little baby steps. My goal is happy, joyous and free. That is where my recovery is taking me, one day at a time.

_____

_____

_____

_____

_____

_____

_____

_____

_____

_____

_____

_____

_____

_____

_____

_____

_____

_____

_____

_____

I Will Never Go Against Myself Again

Today this will be my mantra: I will love my life unconditionally. I will never go against myself again. I will love my life unconditionally. I will never go against myself again.

One definition of sin is to go against yourself. Hurting myself always begins with thoughts: the self-judgments, the obsessions, the anger; they all well up from inside.

Today I will repeat my mantra every fifteen minutes, all day long. I will take responsibility for the messages I give myself. I will love my life unconditionally. I will never go against myself again.

I Have No Idea What I Really Think About the Idea of God

What is sanity? In the second of the 12 steps we say we "came to believe that a power greater than ourselves could restore us to sanity." What am I talking about here? Trying to live up to everyone else's expectations is not sane. I've done that for years, and all I seem to have accomplished is a system of self-judgment and resentment.

Living in my addictions is a graduate school in insanity. Maybe the answer is in that power greater than myself. What I have believed about myself is truly no place to invest my faith, so my perception of myself is not the answer. I see that clearly today. At the same time, I have no idea what I think about the idea of God.

There is no sanity in the world's interpretation of God. Religions have used their claim that God is on their side to persecute, murder and judge for thousands of years. Maybe I'll let that power greater than myself be a mystery. Maybe I don't have to agree to believe anything. My goal is to live my life happy, joyous and free and this can be my power greater than myself. Like they say in the rooms, keep it simple. In truth, I couldn't care less about sanity; I just want to be happy.

I have come to believe that I don't *have* to believe anything right now. I need to take care of me, one day at a time. Sanity today will be not needing an answer. Sanity will be showing up for myself and believing in happy, joyous and free.

I Will Go, Right Now, to the Mirror

The foundations of recovery are honesty, open-mindedness and willingness.

I will go, right now, to the mirror, look into my own eyes and repeat these words: honesty, open-mindedness, willingness.

Feel them.

All that stands between embracing these words and their truth, are those attitudes and habits that I am undoing in my recovery. I am free to create the life of my dreams. As I transform my life, I transform the misery that was my inheritance.

I am worthy of this path. I am a child of the Creator, claiming my birthright of joy, one thought, one choice, one day at a time.

I am grateful for the challenges that freedom offers me. I will unravel all that stands in the way of my recovery. This is my commitment to myself and to life.

I Awoke in a Panic

I've heard people talk about using in dreams, but until last night I hadn't had a dream like that.

I awoke in a panic. The scene and feelings were so real. I was terrified. I was trying to get high and couldn't understand why I wasn't. My mind was going crazy. I felt all the anticipation of using, as well as the guilt.

The power of my addiction is huge. There is so much energy connected to the act of using, or even dreaming of using, that I feel like Jonah being swallowed by the whale. I have a choice in how I perceive this experience. Bottom line, I had a dream about a behavior that I've practiced for years.

I am not powerless over how I respond to the experience. I still have a tremendous amount of feeling and energy connected to the act of using. I can feel the anxiety all through my body.

I have been shown the power the dream had, and I am still sober and present. No judgment is necessary. My mind was running old tapes, tapes that I am reprogramming. I am safe. That is the truth; I am safe.

I realize that recovery is not about fixing my behaviors. Recovery is examining and unraveling the feelings, agreements and reactions that would serve to keep me living in my self-perpetuated hell. I am showing up for myself.

I have a choice in how I react to experiences, whether awake or asleep. I am still sober. I will continue to live my life one situation, one choice, one day at a time.

_____

_____

_____

_____

_____

_____

_____

_____

_____

_____

_____

_____

_____

_____

_____

_____

_____

_____

_____

_____

_____

_____

I Tend to Follow Routines

This morning I am going for a walk. I am going to change my pattern and take a little time for me. All that is required is that I do it.

So, I get out of bed a little early. I don't get caught up in my usual morning ritual, and I get out of the house, one foot in front of the other.

I tend to follow routines. By changing something as simple as my morning routine I can begin my day with a new point of view, and that feels good. This is a great exercise for me in honoring myself and my willingness to be in recovery. I start with the simple things; easy does it.

As I walk I am amazed at how alive I feel. The sights and sounds of the early morning are fresh and vibrant. There is a whole world just outside my door that is new to me. I am new to myself. I love being alive today.

By breaking my old patterns and agreements I am reclaiming the energy that was trapped by those patterns. I am taking back the agreements that held my old life together and using that time and energy to create a new relationship with life. I am taking responsibility for myself.

It is amazing how powerful a simple action like getting out of bed in the morning and taking a walk can be. Recovery is about the little things, one day at a time.

One Hundred and Seventy-Eight Days With No Rain

I awoke last night to the sound of rain.

At first I wasn't sure what the sound was; then suddenly it was familiar.

On the news this morning the weatherperson said it had been 178 days since our last rain. My initial reaction to the rain was disappointment; I had planned a day outside. When I heard that we hadn't had rain in 178 days, I got it—the bigger picture.

Every experience, these days, is a metaphor for my life. What was initially a narrow-minded disappointment about the rain suddenly became gratitude for the bigger picture. Rain brings life to this desert landscape; rain brings life and awareness to me. My disappointment was short-lived when I let go of investment in expectations.

What a gift! I'm not even out of bed yet, and I'm grateful for my newly developed ability to let go of how life "has to look," my gratitude for life taking care of itself.

I am so grateful for my life today, for these opportunities to awaken, for the raindrops. This is life on life's terms, and I get to be a tiny, tiny little part of the whole amazing miracle.

My Faith Was Really Invested in Using

Faith: scary word for me. I have always related faith to religion, judgment, fear.

I was asked today what I had invested my faith in. I couldn't answer because I'm not sure.

For a long time my faith was invested in avoiding the pain of life. All my years of addiction and depression were a response to fear and a lack of trust, of faith, in life.

My faith was really invested in using. For a long time using worked, and then somewhere along the way it didn't anymore. So where does that leave my faith? This is a big question, an important question. There is no right or wrong answer. What is important is that I am willing to go inside myself and feel my way toward my truth.

Whatever my answer, it is nobody else's business, and with each new day my relationship to faith may change.

I am going to take my time with this question. I'll write on it and not cling to any answer, knowing that by simply putting my attention on this relationship to faith the relationship will come to life, growing and evolving.

I am recovering myself today. Sweet and easy does it.

Her Response Was Great

I have a choice in what I believe.

Last night I ran into an old friend, and we sat and talked for a while. As our conversation went along, I realized she appeared to be confused by my point of view. I had not had a conversation with this person for almost a year, not since I began my recovery path. Rather than make an assumption about what she was thinking, I asked her directly, "Are you uncomfortable?" Her response was great. She said she was thinking, as we talked, that she never realized that I had such depth.

The old me would have been offended and defensive; I could feel that reaction in my body, like I was disappointed by her opinion of me. At the same time it felt good.

Knowing that she was seeing a side of me that she didn't recognize was an acknowledgement of the life I live today. I saw so many things clearly. I chose not to be in reaction to old feelings and messages. I made the choice to ask about her apparent anxiety around our conversation, and in her response I was affirmed by her perception of me. She saw that something was different.

I also didn't take her acknowledgement as an ego boost. The situation was simple. I have changed; my life is cleaner and clearer than I can ever remember it being, and that is the result of choices I have made. My reactions are choices. What I believe is a choice. This is very cool. Showing up for myself is changing my life, one day at a time.

Morning Pages

I started reading a book titled *The Artist's Way* the other day. A friend recommended it. At first I didn't have a clue why. The book appeared to be for writers, and I wasn't a writer.

At the beginning of the book there is an exercise called "Morning Pages." The directions are to get out of bed, go immediately to your desk, and write whatever is in your head, your body or your feelings.

The exercise is not about doing it right. The exercise is about clearing your mind.

Not being a writer, I was sure whatever I wrote would be stupid—and that was my sign that I should try this.

I refuse to let petty self-judgments keep me trapped any longer. So I started writing, every day, first thing, just as the author directed.

The process is really cool, and it works. What I have found is that as my morning expressions go on paper I release them. The action of writing offers the stillness of a morning meditation, without having to sit still.

When I stop and take inventory of the practices that bring happiness and fulfillment into my life today I see clearly that by choosing to challenge myself I am freeing myself.

What used to be called comfortable was not comfortable at all; it was only familiar. Today I'm not settling for comfortable. Today I am living, grateful, honest and willing.

The God of My Understanding

"Made a conscious decision to turn our will and our lives over to the care of the God of our understanding." The third step of the twelve steps asks me to surrender my patterns and behaviors, my excuses and justifications, and my determination to be who I think I am, all for faith in something called the God of my understanding. I have tried everything else I know, so why not?

To make a conscious decision means that I am responsible for that decision, that I am committed to my decision and that I will do my best to allow my decision to work for me.

I have no idea what God is. I won't even pretend to know. That seems ridiculous, to believe I would know what God is when I can't even manage to live life without insanity as my closest companion. Being in life is close enough to knowing God for me, and being in life is a full-time responsibility these days.

None of the stuff I thought I knew could get me out of my misery, so having faith in something beyond my knowing feels like a better idea.

As I live with these twelve steps, I will develop my own authentic relationship with them. Listening to others about their relationships with the steps is great, but I will give myself the respect and challenge of having my own relationship with them.

My recovery is about reclaiming myself, and that is what I will remember today.

I Ate in an Indian Restaurant

Last night I ate dinner with friends at an Indian restaurant. My initial reaction when they decided to go to an Indian restaurant was, ummm, no thanks. For some reason, I decided, a long time ago, that I didn't like Indian food. Like so many things in my life, I don't remember how I came to this conclusion.

I am realizing that my life is full of agreements and beliefs that I developed a long time ago, and a lot of them are not true.

My recovery has become about a lot more than the behaviors that got me into recovery in the first place. What I found out last night was that I liked the food. If I had stuck with my initial reaction, I would have missed out on a great evening with friends, and I would have continued to believe something about myself that was not true.

This is a good example of how little I really know about myself, and how much fun I can have getting to know myself again. I am my own creation. I am responsible for what I choose to believe.

What I do know today is that I love being alive. Life has become an adventure, and I am my own lead character. What I believe is my responsibility and my choice.

Today I'll do my best to be aware of my automatic responses, and when they come up I will be willing to challenge myself. If I want to live happy, joyous and free, it is up to me to free myself from all those beliefs that do not serve me today.

Sunday Is a Lazy Family Day

This is Sunday morning. Sunday has always felt unique to me. I grew up with Sunday being a lazy family day. It is interesting how ingrained that old Sunday morning feeling is. Right now it feels a bit lonely and distant. I miss it, kind of once removed, like a cousin you miss and who, at the same time, you wouldn't go out of your way to see.

Memory is powerful. In my recovery, I am well served to remember that. I have all kinds of memories, with all kinds of programming attached to those memories. To be aware of that programming will serve me.

With awareness I can be in the moment, today, here, now. Now is where I'm living. When old memories and feelings push me toward old behaviors, I have meetings and people I can connect with that serve to keep me in the moment. I actually have people in my life I trust to be honest with me. When I ask for help or support, they are there for me.

Most of the time my memories are simply feelings from past experiences. Those feelings come and go. So, here I sit with my Sunday morning personal history, knowing that the past is behind and the present is mine to enjoy as I choose. Being here now, I love it all, and I love myself for showing up for myself. When I do that, show up for myself, the past has no power over me. This is recovery, living with awareness and gratitude, one feeling at a time, one day at a time.

_____

_____

_____

_____

_____

_____

_____

_____

_____

_____

_____

_____

_____

_____

_____

_____

_____

_____

_____

She Was Not Interested in the Truth

How can anyone know me when I don't really know myself? I spoke to an ex yesterday, and she was projecting that sarcastic I-don't-like-you attitude. How she feels is her business. As we talked, she asked about being in recovery, and it was clear she was asking questions she already had her own answers for. She was not interested in the truth. She was absorbed in her opinions and attitudes.

At one point I told her how powerful it was, getting to know myself again. Her reply was quick—she knew who I was. Instantly, I realized she wasn't talking to me, she was talking to her own judgments and opinions.

I told her I had to go and walked away.

I was overwhelmed with feelings. Not good enough, unfaithful, a disappointment, all these feelings flew into my face. I went straight to my old familiar hell. I reminded myself that what someone else believes about me has little to do with me. My history with my ex was just that, history. I am not willing to trash today over what was done.

I can make amends, but I will not participate in someone else's replay of our past. My recovery is for me. I am cleaning up my life and reclaiming my integrity for myself. Who I am is what I am becoming. I don't need more of a definition. Before I can define myself I have to be myself, and who I am changes daily. So, who would a definition serve? Being present, alive and aware is the gift I give myself today.

_____

_____

_____

_____

_____

_____

_____

_____

_____

_____

_____

_____

_____

_____

_____

_____

_____

_____

_____

Even At My Craziest

There is a lot about this recovery process that I didn't expect. My latest awareness is food. Even at my craziest I paid some attention to how I ate. I always remembered the "you are what you eat" pitch.

Today I experienced a direct connection between the way I eat and the way I feel. I am aware of the subtleties of my energy level and my ability to focus—both affected by diet. The truth is that I care about how I feel, and the food I eat has an impact on that.

Taking care of myself means just that. What began as addressing my living habits, dealing with self-destructive behaviors, has shifted to taking positive actions like being conscious of my eating.

This is not about worrying about how much I weigh or the self-criticism of how I think I look. This is much simpler and cleaner. This is about how I feel, energetically and physically. I like taking care of myself today.

My point of view has shifted from dealing with the bad me to taking care of myself because I like myself. That's a big deal. I matter to myself now. I realize the difference between taking care of myself out of love rather than taking care of myself out of fear. It is truly a miracle how much my experience of life has changed since I started showing up for myself. Sometimes it is the little things that offer us the greatest gifts.

I do love living my life honestly, with an open mind, with a will.

Today is "Give Myself a Break" Day

If I am cranky, I will just be cranky. At least it's authentic.

I will not pretend today to be something or some way I am not. I will just be myself, in whatever form that is.

My experience is that when I accept myself fully in whatever shape I am in, it helps eliminate stress. I try so hard to "do it right," and that's a lot of pressure. If I just do it the way I am doing it, without judging myself for the right or wrong of it, I feel relieved.

Change will come because I want it to, but I have to be okay with whatever is going on right now, each day, one day at a time.

Expectations Have Ruled My Life

Expectations.

As a child I lived with the expectations of my family. Then I moved on to trying to live up to the expectations of my peers and my school. Looking back, it is amazing to realize how I have lived subject to the power of expectations. Even in recovery I have allowed myself to be defined by how well I met the expectations of my friends and sponsor.

That entire setup just does not work anymore. I am not going to judge myself by the expectations of others. I am going to make my choices based on how I feel. Recovery is offering me the opportunity to live in authentic relationship with myself. Authenticity requires that I be completely responsible for my choices, without judgment.

I will listen to those I respect, and I will make my choices. I am responsible for the choices I make, whether I acknowledge that truth or not. The only way for me to gain confidence in myself is to be myself. I can always choose again.

All Kinds of Reactions
and Judgments

Yesterday was Election Day. Today there are all kinds of reactions and judgments. I've listened to friends talk about what the country needs for change to happen.

It's interesting to see how people believe that change comes from the top. The population of any country is made up of individuals like you and me. What I have learned about myself is that change really happens from the bottom up. I can change partners, houses, jobs, and that does not change who I am inside, which is where the true experience of my life happens.

Through my recovery I have made major changes on the inside. My beliefs, feelings and behaviors have all changed dramatically because I have taken responsibility for myself. Changing appearances does not change the truth. Addressing my life with honesty, open-mindedness and willingness empowers me to change my truth.

As long as my attention was focused on the world outside of myself, nothing really changed. The moment I turned my attention to myself I was offered real choices that could transform my life. I wonder what might happen in this country if all of those so invested in politics put that same attention and energy into themselves. In my own way I feel that my life's journey has offered me the opportunity to wake up as a human being in a way that so-called normal people don't get at all, and I wouldn't trade places with them for the world.

_____

_____

_____

_____

_____

_____

_____

_____

_____

_____

_____

_____

_____

_____

_____

_____

_____

_____

_____

_____

A Searching and Fearless Moral Inventory

Step four: "Made a searching and fearless moral inventory of ourselves." The fourth step of the twelve steps is the powerful act of practicing honesty without self-judgment. What I've done, I've done; it is what it is. I will not live in judgment of the past. What I will do is own all of it. To know myself, I have to look at myself.

Where I've been and what I've done are no longer who I am. My inventory of myself is taking responsibility for my actions, beliefs and behaviors. Before I can let anything go, I have to accept it, own it, see the choices I've made for what they were. My inventory is not a book of judgment; it is an act of recapitulation, an act of personal courage and power. As I write out my inventory, I will be aware of my automatic tendency to judge or defend myself, and I will not indulge in either.

This is an inventory, not judgment day. I will use the steps to work for me, not against me. I am showing up for myself today, and that is a miracle in itself. One day at a time.

_____

_____

_____

_____

_____

_____

_____

_____

_____

_____

_____

_____

_____

_____

_____

_____

_____

_____

_____

Being Awake to the Choices

The wind is blowing like crazy, must be sixty miles an hour. Lying in bed this morning, I thought about my ability to hear the messages of life. Sometimes those messages can be subtle, and I am immediately aware of them. Sometimes subtlety doesn't get my attention. My recovery has allowed me to become aware of the subtleties.

Like the wind, life moves all around me all the time. For years I only recognized life's presence by my resistance to it. Like the wind in the trees, life had to shake my branches pretty hard to get me to look up. My attention was so absorbed in thinking, or emotions, that I lived a day late and a dollar short, as the old saying goes.

Today I know the difference between awake in life and asleep in life. Being awake in life shows me the choices before I am up to my ears in consequences. It is the consequences that led to needing to medicate. It was the medicating that became my addiction.

Sleeping through life is a hard way to go. I tried it. This morning I am awake. I hear that wind blowing, and I am listening. That feels good, just to be present and aware. I am working it, and working it is giving me back my life, one day at a time.

_____

_____

_____

_____

_____

_____

_____

_____

_____

_____

_____

_____

_____

_____

_____

_____

_____

_____

_____

_____

Mr. Stupid Meets Mr. Mouth

Last night I caught myself in a reaction that seemed to come out of nowhere. The reaction was automatic. Somebody said something that hooked me, and *zappo*, I was angry. From that point on I was on automatic pilot, like a crazy person, arguing, determined to be right. Mr. Stupid meets Mr. Mouth, and they're off. Just when I thought I was above all that.

Crazy! Crazy is so ingrained in me. Looking back, at least I can see how the event played out. That's some progress, just the awareness of how I got hooked. The truth is I still have an inventory of automatic opinions and reactions that will completely overrule sanity. There is no need to judge myself over that, which, of course, would be just another automatic . . .

Ahhh! I am paying attention to myself. Today I take responsibility for my actions and reactions, and I will make a phone call and apologize for my behavior. My apology will have no need or expectation of a response from the other person. This is not about the other person. This is about me. I will find my way to happy, joyous and free, and I will do my best, one day at a time.

The Power of Choice
Is the Key to Recovery

A friend of mine quit his job yesterday. We had worked together for a while, and we both enjoyed what we were doing. There was some issue between him and his supervisor, and he got upset and quit.

The cool thing was that last night he called to tell me that he knew he had quit in an emotional reaction, and he didn't want there to be any unresolved feelings between us over what had happened. He told me he had also called his supervisor and made amends and that they were okay with each other. That's how the awareness of recovery works when you work it.

By taking responsibility for himself my friend kept his life clear of resentments, and he showed how truth in action really serves life. The whole situation was simplified and put to rest in one smooth choice of action.

The power of choice, that is the key to recovery. Sometimes seeing recovery work around me is clearer than seeing it happening in my own life. I love it. I'll remember this lesson to help me keep my life clean and honest.

If I'm Not Recovering Who I am, I'm Not Recovering the Truth

I went to a meeting today. As the sharing moved around the room, I became aware that I had a different point of view from the people speaking out. It was not about right or wrong. The truth was that the group's view didn't fit for me; so I told my truth. I could feel the resistance and reaction to what I presented. The voices in my head wanted to put the others down for not being open-minded. Maybe I was just afraid of not being accepted.

Wanting to be accepted has led me to abandon my truth for most of my life, and I will not do that anymore. If I'm not recovering who I really am, I'm not recovering the truth. Sharing my truth out of authenticity is the work of recovery. Sharing my opinion as a reaction to others is poison. I know the difference, and I will do my best to be responsible for the place I choose to speak from. Find your truth, and truth will set you free.

I'm Ready to Push My Comfort Zone

Today, all day, in conversation with others I will look the person I'm talking to in the eye. I am ready to push my comfort zone. I believe that if I'm not comfortable looking someone in the eye, then I'm not comfortable with myself. I like myself today, so I may as well show up in conversation. This will be a great exercise in just witnessing the voices in my head while staying present in my commitment to myself. I think that is enough for today. Easy does it, eye to eye.

When I Feel Good Physically, It Is Easy to Be Happy

As soon as I finish my morning writing, I am going to work out. That might be going surfing or going to the gym. Maybe I'll just take a long walk; whatever I do I am doing something to take care of my body. After all the years of neglecting my body I know today that my entire presence in life is subject to the attention I give it.

When I feel good physically, it is easy to be happy. The more energy I have the more living I can do, and living is really what recovery is about. By focusing on my well-being I am focusing on loving myself. It has taken me a while to come to terms with the idea of loving myself; that always seemed strange to me. I wasn't against loving myself; I just had no idea what it would look like.

Then one day I realized that getting my body back in shape was loving myself. Keep it simple. I am constantly made aware of how little I really know about loving the life I live, and I'm having a great time figuring that out. Showing up for myself has made all the difference.

Let Go of Suffering, and You Won't Need the Medicators

The biggest wounds in my life continued to haunt me because I stayed stuck to them. Things that happened years ago remained alive and miserable in my mind because I identified myself by them. That's the truth. I didn't know any better. It's no wonder I needed to medicate; I'd been haunting myself.

As long as I see myself as a victim I will find a way to be victimized. What an amazing and empowering realization! I can change so much when I am willing to see my life from a different point of view. (I have finally gotten to the place where I don't care what I think about my realizations. What matters is how I choose to use them.) I am the one who built my life around suffering, and I am the only one who can undo that addiction to suffering.

Let go of the suffering, and I won't need the medicators. This is progress. Keep coming back; it works if you work it.

An Opportunity to Look Deep

"Admitted to God, to ourselves and to another human being the exact nature of our wrongs." The fifth step of the twelve steps is an opportunity to look deep into the mirror of another person's eyes and be accountable for our actions. This is not about judgment; judgment is part of the problem, not the solution. Working the fifth step is an act of honesty about the past, a willingness to step through the personal importance of guilt and shame, and the open-mindedness of allowing life to work its magic through us.

By my admission I set the intention to let go of all that is attached to the baggage of my past. That baggage no longer serves me, and I will no longer identify myself by it. By my working these steps I am giving myself the gift of creating my own authentic relationship with the steps and with life. I am recovering my willingness to be who I choose. Through honesty, open-mindedness and willingness I am opening the doorway to my personal freedom.

READER/CUSTOMER CARE SURVEY

HEFG

We care about your opinions! Please take a moment to fill out our online Reader Survey at **http://survey.hcibooks.com**.
As a **"THANK YOU"** you will receive a **VALUABLE INSTANT COUPON** towards future book purchases as well as a **SPECIAL GIFT** available
only online! Or, you may mail this card back to us and we will send you a copy of our exciting catalog with your valuable coupon inside.

(PLEASE PRINT IN ALL CAPS)

First Name   MI.   Last Name

Address

City

State   Zip   Email

1. Gender
❑ Female   ❑ Male

2. Age
❑ 8 or younger
❑ 9-12   ❑ 13-16
❑ 17-20   ❑ 21-30
❑ 31+

3. Did you receive this book as a gift?
❑ Yes   ❑ No

4. Annual Household Income
❑ under $25,000
❑ $25,000 - $34,999
❑ $35,000 - $49,999
❑ $50,000 - $74,999
❑ over $75,000

5. What are the ages of the children living in your house?
❑ 0 - 14   ❑ 15+

6. Marital Status
❑ Single
❑ Married
❑ Divorced
❑ Widowed

7. How did you find out about the book?
(please choose one)
❑ Recommendation
❑ Store Display
❑ Online
❑ Catalog/Mailing
❑ Interview/Review

8. Where do you usually buy books?
(please choose one)
❑ Bookstore
❑ Online
❑ Book Club/Mail Order
❑ Price Club (Sam's Club, Costco's, etc.)
❑ Retail Store (Target, Wal-Mart, etc.)

9. What subject do you enjoy reading about the most?
(please choose one)
❑ Parenting/Family
❑ Relationships
❑ Recovery/Addictions
❑ Health/Nutrition
❑ Christianity
❑ Spirituality/Inspiration
❑ Business Self-help
❑ Women's Issues
❑ Sports

10. What attracts you most to a book?
(please choose one)
❑ Title
❑ Cover Design
❑ Author
❑ Content

TAPE IN MIDDLE; DO NOT STAPLE

NO POSTAGE
NECESSARY
IF MAILED
IN THE
UNITED STATES

BUSINESS REPLY MAIL
FIRST-CLASS MAIL PERMIT NO 45 DEERFIELD BEACH, FL

POSTAGE WILL BE PAID BY ADDRESSEE

Health Communications, Inc.
3201 SW 15th Street
Deerfield Beach FL 33442-9875

FOLD HERE

Comments

I Was Suddenly Grateful for My Life Today

They were pictures from the past. As I turned the pages all those old feelings came alive, like water rising slowly with the tide. The time that has passed since those photographs were taken seemed suddenly irrelevant. I was completely absorbed in memories. Sad, sweet, all those what-ifs.

That's when I caught myself. I saw the me now connected to the me then. As my awareness came back into the moment I was suddenly grateful for my life today. I was also grateful for my life then and all the rest in between. Life is living through me, in me. What might have been a wallowing in pity and sadness became a gift of gratitude for all that has happened by offering myself back to the truth of life in recovery.

Those old stories are just stories now, the memories, just memories. To be grateful for life without the judgments and old scores is freedom. I am here today, and maybe I'll be here tomorrow, and all that happens in between, well, that's between me and life.

Life Happens After Dark, Sober

Last night was the first time in a long time that I was out until two A.M. I was amazed at the whole scene, hanging out with friends in a club, listening to a great band, sober. I really had a good time. Before we went out, I was scared. I don't think I ever left a club sober before. I'm not sure the last time I arrived sober. That's almost funny.

Life does happen sober after dark. Amazing. I only decided to go because I was going with friends who don't get high and who had a lot more recovery time than I had. I was careful, and I thought out my choice to join them.

Once again the way I am now making my decisions makes sense, and it's working for me. Recovery is about living life. Last night was recovery working for me, and me working with it. We're making progress here. Thank you everybody who's come before. I appreciate your honesty, your willingness and your open-mindedness. Peace be with you.

_____
_____
_____
_____
_____
_____
_____
_____
_____
_____
_____
_____
_____
_____
_____
_____
_____
_____
_____
_____
_____
_____

The Real Me Is Alive and Getting Well

For a long time now I've been afraid to set any goals or intentions for myself. I've been doing my best to just stay in the moment and not get carried away by reactions or fears. Being present in the moment has felt good and safe. Actually feeling safe and sober was reward enough. I realize now that I want to set a longer-term plan for my life. I can trust myself more today, and I know I can follow through on my intentions. I've done it; I'm sober.

Looking at my life I want to pursue the dreams lost in the chaos of my past. Those old dreams were the real me, and the real me is alive and getting well today. It's time for me to make a list of intentions and goals, starting with short term and projecting out a couple years.

To be able to look at my life and feel excited about possibilities is a miracle, and this miracle I've given myself. I know that even as I make my list and set my goals I will not get trapped by the form. My goals are about the quality of my life and being authentic and true to myself.

That's what I'll remember as I make my list and set my intentions. The rest is between me and the Creator and life.

All I have to do is keep showing up, one day at a time.

_____

_____

_____

_____

_____

_____

_____

_____

_____

_____

_____

_____

_____

_____

_____

_____

_____

_____

_____

_____

_____

Lighten Up, Man!

I was looking at myself in the mirror today and suddenly realized that I am not this body. I saw my body as a vehicle, like a mobile home. I started laughing when the voice in my head started sounding like a car salesman, "Well, he's got a few miles on him, but the motor was rebuilt just last year, and it's running real good these days."

I've come a long way in not taking myself so seriously. I must have been a little kid the last time I could entertain myself with my own sense of humor. Even in recovery, there is a tendency to be too self-indulgent. I'm going to let that one go today. I'm going to laugh with myself at this crazy world we live in. I'm going to "let go and let God" as they say in the rooms. Lighten up, man. There you go. Easy does it. It's a good thing there is no lemon law for humans, or I'm sure I'd have sent myself back to the factory a long time ago. Peace!

Magical and Mysterious Work for Me

I see crows and ravens everywhere. I just heard one outside. I started to pay attention to them while I was in treatment. Maybe they were around before; I don't know. I remember looking them up in an animal spirit book to find out what seeing ravens and crows was supposed to mean, and not ten minutes later three of them flew right over my head.

I knew then that the description in the book was the author's perception, and I had to find my own. Then I felt my answer. Ravens and crows are here to remind me that life is magical and mysterious, and only fools waste time trying to figure it out.

Okay, so I've been a fool. Big deal! Magical and mysterious work for me. Today I'm going to let life be life and not indulge in trying to figure out squat. The mystery has offered me the freedom of recovering myself, and the magic is that the crows and ravens are helping to remind me how far I've come. This life is teaching me, and I am so willing to learn. That's my relationship with recovery, honesty, open-mindedness, willingness and awareness.

Knowing Is Not Believing:
Knowing Is Knowing

I read a book where one of the characters in the story was asked, "What do you know?" As he responded, it was pointed out that what this guy thought he knew, in truth, was only what he believed.

Since I began my recovery journey, I have addressed all the beliefs that I had accepted as truths, but weren't. Undoing those distorted beliefs has freed me from the lies that kept me bound and defensive. Knowing is not believing. Beliefs change with the wind. Beliefs demand being defended when challenged. Knowing is truth.

Beliefs are volumes of information, definition and expectation. For years, the few things I knew about myself were buried beneath the stuff I had come to *believe* about myself. Even addressing this awareness could not have happened before I found the clarity of sobriety.

My freedom matters today. The joy of life matters today. I *know* that. What I believe, well, that's the fuel for lots of conversation.

I have a self-assignment to write down what I think I know, and once a week examine that list. I add to and erase from it as I go. It's about keeping myself accountable for what I accept as the truth in my life.

Life will show me the difference between believing and knowing. I had no idea that I could have so much fun investigating myself! It works if you work it.

I Used to Be Paranoid

I just remembered I used to be paranoid. I used to be as paranoid as a turtle in a crosswalk. My life has changed so much so fast since I let go of trying to make it fit into a box. The whole idea of how I used to be is funny. Like some whacked black comedy. *The Man from Bizarro World*, that would be me.

Recovery is about the process. Like they say in the rooms, "Progress, not perfection." Perfection used to be something I held myself in judgment against. Now the idea of perfection is ridiculous and boring. I don't need to be perfect; life is perfect, and I've got myself a piece of that action. I am busy living today.

The judge that used to preside over my life has taken a seat in the back of my mind. Every once in a while he demands attention, being the obnoxious character that he is, but I let whatever he has to say go because I don't care.

When I fired my judge, my victim got so offended that he took a seat next to him. Perfect. See there, perfection does exist, just beyond expectation. I don't know where my paranoia went, and again I don't care. What I do know is that when I was willing to let my insanity go, really let it go, it went. All I had to do was keep showing up and keep my attention focused on the moment. There are miracles waiting to happen; all we have to do is get out of the way.

It's About Letting Go

"Were entirely ready to have God remove all these defects of character." The sixth step of the twelve steps is about letting go. The first time I worked the sixth step, I believed that the step was literal. I believed that when I was "ready" God would do the job for me. That didn't work very well.

My first reaction was not to believe the step, as if the step had some meaning other than whatever meaning I had given it. Today I know what I needed to disbelieve was my interpretation. So I tried again, being less literal and more responsible. My defects of character all came down to my beliefs about myself. I created those beliefs, and I agreed with them, so it was up to me to change them.

To have my "defects of character" removed is not based on self-judgment. Removing those defects is about letting go of anything that limits the joy and creativity in my life. Learning the power of letting go is an amazing gift, one that I use on a daily basis. I am becoming aware of my tendency to attach to beliefs as though they were answers.

All of my character defects are connected to what, at some point in my life, were acceptable answers for me. The sixth step is taking responsibility for the old inventory of answers and behaviors. My letting go is me recovering my truth today.

Spontaneity Is the Doorway to Creativity

Go to your stereo or radio. Put on your favorite song. Don't think, just do it. Sit down and listen, hear it all, all the tones, all the players, all the magic. If your body wants to move, then move it. Be free, right now in this moment. There is no need to say anything to anybody; you have the right to do this. No explanations.

Spontaneity is the doorway to creativity, and recovery is creativity in action. We are on this planet for a reason, and living life is the reason. I love myself today. I love you today. Crank it up!

_____

_____

_____

_____

_____

_____

_____

_____

_____

_____

_____

_____

_____

_____

_____

_____

_____

_____

_____

_____

_____

It Is Time I Began to Trust Myself

My mind has been the operations-center of my life. Over the years I've read many books and listened to many teachers that offered points of view and opinions about our relationship with life and the world. All of that information has fed into my way of thinking and perceiving. Some of that information I did not believe, and a lot of it I did. The same process has been happening in my recovery.

From the rooms, to my sponsor, to therapists, doctors and friends, there is always someone offering an opinion about what or how I should be in recovery. I have been too willing to listen and then compare their points of view to mine, either agreeing or disagreeing with them. When I agreed, it felt good; when I disagreed, I told myself a story about why I was right and they weren't. I have continued to be invested in others agreeing with me.

It is time I began to trust myself. In sobriety I can change my mind and my decisions in a heartbeat. In a heartbeat I can use or not. Regardless of whether I choose to see the truth or not, my recovery is based on my willingness to be honest with myself. I cannot give that responsibility to anyone else, and no one else can assume it. Today my relationship with my thinking, with my mind, is also my responsibility.

Today I will be aware of the stories I tell myself, and I will be responsible for what I believe and don't believe about my stories.

Our Culture Is Obsessed with Sex

Sex is a natural aspect of our being. Using sex as a refuge from our fear and loneliness is a manipulation. As with all the other areas of my life, I am responsible for my relationship with my sexuality. There are so many distortions and judgments attached to sex that I find myself moving very slowly and consciously toward my truth in relationship with it.

Our culture is obsessed with sex. Most religions are obsessed with sex. Everywhere I go, sex, and all the games that are played in relation to it, seems to occupy a big part of most people's lives. I am tired of the poison that comes from the judgments. I am also tired of sex hooking my attention and my mind, entertaining the fantasy that the right partner or relationship could fix my life.

What I know today is that most of my adult relationships were the result of my woundedness seeking refuge. No wonder there were always problems. I was the problem. Recovery is about me as a whole being. Healing me will affect all of my relationships in life, especially my most intimate ones. Knowing that makes it easier to remind myself to slow down.

What's the hurry? The healthier and happier I get the cooler my relationships will be. I'll remember that today. Slow down; easy does it.

_____

_____

_____

_____

_____

_____

_____

_____

_____

_____

_____

_____

_____

_____

_____

_____

_____

_____

_____

I Am Responsible for My Behavior

I have two daughters who have lived through the misery of having an addicted parent. I have let them down and broken their hearts. I am responsible for my behavior. I hate what I have done to them.

The past is done. There is nothing I can do about that. What I can do, I am doing. I am responsible for my behavior. I have taken responsibility for myself.

Recovery is not about changing the past. Recovery is about healing the past and living in the moment. What I am doing for myself today is as powerful, in a positive sense, as the choices of the past were hurtful. I am showing my children that we can do whatever we choose in our lives.

The greatest gift I can give them now is to be honest, open-minded and willing to allow them to be themselves. As I take care of myself, I'm showing them that life is the result of the choices we make, and each of us is responsible for our own choices. Maybe the gift I am giving them now will be greater than the hurt that I've caused them. I hope so.

The sadness over the past is still there and so is the promise of the future. The truth is we are recovering together, and they don't even know that's my gift to them.

Thank you, Life, for the opportunity to be more than the sum of my past.

I Am Here

As I prayed this morning, a voice spoke softly in my mind.

"I am here."

"Who are you?" I quickly asked. There was only silence and stillness. That was the answer, the stillness of peace. In the silence was the answer to all the questions I've ever had about who I am. The stillness touched me, and I listened. The true inspiration in my life today comes from completely unexpected places.

I would never have dreamed that in silence I would find the answer to so many questions. Life surrounds us offering itself as a choice. Today I will listen for the meaning within the stillness. I will listen beyond the noise of thought and reaction.

Today I will walk with my prayers.

Humility Is the Opposite of Personal Importance

"Humbly asked God to remove our shortcomings." The seventh step of the twelve steps allows us the opportunity to let go of our resistance to asking for help. Humility is the opposite of personal importance, and personal importance is an obstacle to freedom.

The removal of my shortcomings has been a team effort. When I have been ready and willing to let go, life has taken away what I've offered. My shortcomings don't serve me any longer, so offering them back to life only makes sense.

On second thought, the act of humbly asking is serving me, so even dealing with shortcomings becomes an action of personal power.

In recovery I am finding good in places I would never have expected it. I am finding a courage and willingness in myself that I didn't know I had, and I am learning to love living life again, one day at a time.

The Level of Honesty
Recovery Demands

Telling my truth all the time is a real challenge. Telling my truth all the time is the level of honesty that my recovery demands. I compromise myself by worrying about how others might react to my honesty. The reactions of others are not my responsibility; being true to myself is.

This point of view is ruthless, and it is necessary if I'm going to free myself from the insanity of my past. This is my commitment to myself today. I will be completely honest in all my words and deeds.

"God grant me the serenity to accept the things I cannot change, the courage to change the things I can, and the wisdom to know the difference,"* and the willingness to take action!

---

* "The Serenity Prayer," Reinhold Niebuhr

Heartbreak Was My Best Old Friend

"Ain't no sunshine when she's gone. . . ." The sound track of my life had a lot of old heartbreak songs woven through it. Heartbreak was one of my best old friends. We lived, worked and played together. We also got loaded and miserable together. I used heartbreak as an excuse for so long that one day it got fed up with me, and I just went numb. The party was over.

It was the numbness that led to recovery. The other side of numb was dead, and I was not willing to go that far. Looking back it is clear now that all my old heartbreaks were the truth trying to get through to me, that I was choosing my own mirrors. Heartbreak is the mirror of truth. Heartbreak is life showing us that there is no love in our expectations.

Love is found in freedom, and freedom is love without conditions. Realizing the truth and living it takes practice. That is what my recovery will be about today, my willingness to practice living in the truth without conditions.

_____

_____

_____

_____

_____

_____

_____

_____

_____

_____

_____

_____

_____

_____

_____

_____

_____

_____

Gossip Is a Choice

I get so tired of listening to gossip. There seems to be a disease afflicting humans that feeds off of our poisoned opinions not only of others but ourselves as well. I can be having a great day, and I'll fall into listening to someone's opinion of me. I'll immediately go on the defensive or react in anger or agree and take on the opinion as though it were the truth. Not trusting myself is the setup to being vulnerable to the poison of others.

I have good cause not to trust myself. That's why I'm working my recovery. Participating in gossip is a choice; ~~and so is not participating.~~ If I do not involve myself in gossip, I will develop my own immunity to it. Any poison I stir up about someone else has to pass through me first.

I'm not willing to do that. My recovery will give me back my faith in myself; that is just a matter of time. This awareness is a big part of working my program, and like they say, it works if you work it.

Today I'll stay out of and away from gossip, period.

Living Is the Point

I'm going on a road trip like the old days, load up, fill up and drive. I need some space and some wind in my face. Living life not out of control gives me a lot of options. You know what, life is going by here. Living is the point; so go have some fun.

I've Not Allowed for the Mystery

I've always had expectations about how things should turn out or what the results should look like. I see today how I have only limited myself by thinking life should unfold according to my book of demands. I've not allowed for any mystery in life's unfolding. Taking this awareness one step further reinforces the truth that I have lived the results of my own choosing. My life is my creation. I've been directing this show.

From now on I'm going to do my best not to allow my expectations to get in the way of life's mystery. I'll make my choices from the heart, not out of questionable thinking. This also requires that I get over taking myself so seriously. That alone should make room for a lot more fun. Easy does it in action, that's my commitment for today, with no expectations.

My Body Says: Pay Attention!

I am finding it interesting how subtle the messages my body conveys can be. In the beginning my recovery allowed me to actually feel the physical transformation that was happening. As I got clean from using, I could really feel my body again.

I knew I needed to start taking care of my body. Recovery is about all of me. So I started walking more and trying things like yoga and going to the gym. I was ashamed of the truth of my physical condition, and I was determined to take responsibility for that.

Some months have passed now, and I am in better shape. I feel better and look better. Lately I've realized that I am also sensitive to the food I eat.

Again my body is telling me that I need to pay attention to it. My body has no agenda other than its own well-being, so it only makes sense to listen.

This is my commitment: I will not do the drive-through window thing. I will eat fresh, balanced meals. I am going to start cooking more, invite friends over and share some meals together.

By putting my attention on physical well-being and making it fun to take care of myself it will be easy to follow through. Sweet and simple, that's what I'm practicing today. Recovery is what I make of it. One day at a time.

_____

_____

_____

_____

_____

_____

_____

_____

_____

_____

_____

_____

_____

_____

_____

_____

_____

_____

The Ancient Symbol of Infinity

"Made a list of the persons we had harmed, and became willing to make amends to them all." By acknowledging my past actions I am taking responsibility for those actions. To free myself from the old patterns of guilt, shame and blame, I have to walk through my resistance to being honest with myself.

It must not be a coincidence that this eighth step of the twelve steps is also the ancient symbol of infinity. The gift of acting on the eighth step is the freedom that is life itself.

My greatest reward in working through my list is in freeing myself from feeling the guilt, fear and shame that comes up when I cross paths with the people I've harmed.

From that point of view, you could say that working step eight is a selfish act, because I am the one who benefits from my actions. My recovery is by me, for me.

As I transform, I reclaim the truth that will set me free, one day at a time.

My Mom Did the Best She Could

Today is Mother's Day. I was just thinking about my mother and the life she's lived. I inherited a lot of beliefs and attitudes from my mom. Some of them I was conscious of, and some I'm just now realizing.

We learn an entire reality from our parents. My mom did the best she could, and I'm grateful for that. As a recovering person I've been offered the opportunity to see how I've chosen to use what I learned as a child. As an adult I have the ability to let go of what no longer serves me.

The agreements that I live by today are my responsibility, and none of those agreements are sacred. I will question all of them from time to time. This awareness is my gift to my mother. Having taken all I learned growing up, I'm finally making it authentic, and I am releasing anything that goes against my truth.

Willingness to take responsibility for the life I live is my gift to life, the mother of us all. On this Mother's Day I will share gratitude with everyone I touch. Throughout the day, I'll acknowledge all of those people and places that have nurtured my life. All of those relationships are alive here within me. Today I will walk softly upon this earth, remembering that we are all born of the body of the Mother. Peace be with you.

The Hurt Is In My Expectations

It is important that I be honest about those things that hurt me. My tendency has always been to turn my hurt inward. When I do that, I create resentments and live with anger. That does not work for me now. To have the courage to express myself creates a mirror for my feelings. I've learned that most of the situations that hurt me are not about the other person. The hurt is in my own expectations and my self-judgments.

The people in my life have the right to choose whatever they like, and so do I. From that point of view I will grant the freedom to others that I want for myself. There is no place for hurt when I live with respect for the choices of others. What I will get back is the reminder of how precious my freedom of choice is to me.

We Live in a World of Cause and Effect

There are two aspects to this world. There is the physical world, and there is the world of spirit, the essence of creation. Our lives are a continuously evolving dance between the two. As we experience life we process our experiences, which then influence our future perceptions and beliefs.

Humans learn through experience. Recovery is a process of becoming aware of, and responsible for, our relationship with experience. We live in a world of action-reaction, cause and effect. As we believe, so we create.

Personal freedom is the ability to live in the moment, with awareness of our past and all of our beliefs and opinions, and not be at the mercy of our reactions. Recovery is about evolving beyond the limitations of our past.

This is my prayer for today: Creator, grant me the serenity to see myself apart from my beliefs and opinions. Allow me the opportunity to see myself as evolution, as your creation moving with awareness toward the grace of happy, joyous and free.

Ask for What You Need

Since I began my recovery journey, I have been learning to ask for what I need. In the past I believed that it was selfish to ask for what I needed. Today I know that taking care of myself is my primary responsibility. To ask for what I need is simple; I just do it. The person I'm asking can always say no. I will respect the answer whatever it is.

The same truth applies to others asking something of me. I can say "yes" or "no" without obligation. It takes courage and open-mindedness to ask for what I need and not attach conditions to the asking. What a great exercise for recovery, to be willing to stretch myself and my comfort zone.

Awareness and acceptance are the keys to freedom. Courage is the force that lights my way.

I Want My Relationships to Be Honest

To see others as they are, without judgment, is an act of love. Allowing the people in my life to be who they are is exactly what I would ask of them. I want my relationships to be honest. If I don't take others' opinions personally, then they cannot hurt me. In all of my relationships I will give what I would ask for myself—the truth.

Facing the Past Is Facing Our Beliefs

Step nine: "Made direct amends to such people wherever possible, except when to do so would injure them or others." Step nine is the fulfillment of step eight. Facing our past is facing our beliefs about ourselves. We can't change what we are not willing to acknowledge, and acknowledging our past requires taking action.

What I have to be careful of in making my amends is my responsibility to those who might be affected by my actions. I do not want to add to the baggage at hand or do more harm.

This is not about getting out of responsibility by passing poison along to someone else. This is about me cleaning up my history and relationships with others and taking back any poison I may have put on others that did not belong to them.

Recovery is about taking action, responsibly with love and compassion for all.

Living With Awareness

What I know today is that nothing is for sure. Knowing that life is a mystery offers the opportunity to always stay aware of myself, as well as the world around me. When I live with awareness in each moment I am always present for myself. My power of choice and intention are my greatest tools. This is life living through me, without expectation. Recovering presence in the moment is my commitment to recovery today.

As I breathe in the air and light of this morning I am breathing in life—sober, present, grateful and aware.

In Recovery, the Truth
Is My Greatest Ally

The point of life is living. Recovery is reclaiming the power to create a life of choice. In my addiction I chose according to the distortions of my disease. Those distortions were self-perpetuating. An addiction is a pattern of belief and behavior that feeds on our fear of seeing our true selves. In recovery the truth is my greatest ally.

Like the sword in the stone, the gift of our true inheritance as the children of creation is embedded in the rock of time, awaiting our return to integrity. Only in our integrity will we be able to pull the sword of truth free from the stone.

In many traditions this journey is seen as a warrior's path. Through the eyes of the sacred mother, recovery is the awakening of the sleeping heart. There is no right way to see this transformation. Our point of view is just that, ours, and we each have one. Through willingness to question the suffering that plagues us we will each find our own way back to our truth. Find your truth, and the truth will set you free.

From this day forward, "I will live my life with gratitude, love, loyalty and justice, beginning with myself and continuing with my brothers and sisters."* I will walk in beauty as the beauty of life surrounds me. My commitment is to myself, to my life and to my Creator, one day at a time.

---

*Don Miguel Ruiz

An Anchor in the Present

"Continued to take personal inventory, and when we were wrong promptly admitted it." For all of my focus on my past, and the power and grace of healing that past, my life is still being lived in the moment. Step ten of the twelve steps is an anchor in the present. The unraveling of my old baggage will not accomplish much if I am not keeping my house in order today.

To be in relationship with my choices is not an act of judging myself. My choices are subject to my ability to own and direct them. As I move through life I will be constantly aware of the feelings connected to the choices at hand. Those feelings are honest, so I will listen to them.

As I reclaim my integrity, my ability to choose will become more fluid and creative. By being responsible for my inventory, I will immediately undo any agreements or actions that go against my integrity.

Working these steps is opening the door to freedom, and I am showing up for the occasion.

Ease and Grace Will Be With Me

Today is beautiful. The sky, the clouds, the light filtering through feed my soul. I am at peace. I realize in these moments that it is peace and recognition of the beauty that surrounds me that I have longed for.

I am in the space that holds peace, whispering: "Remember . . . remember." I do not need to think right now. Thinking cannot improve on this moment. Look around. Do you see that all insanity exists in the minds of humans?

That has been me—suffering from an affliction of my own creation. Not now. I will let the quiet offer its truth. Learning not to believe the voices of my mind, or the world, lets me feel my way into what is true for me. I love being alive. Taking care of myself today will be easy.

Ease and grace will be with me. Peace be with you.

I Feel a Surge of Energy

The last three days it has rained. Thick, heavy clouds have hung in the sky like shadows from the past. Then, this morning, I awoke to an incredible blue, sun-filled sky. What a relief!

I felt a surge of energy seeing the light pour into my windows. I seem to be more in sync with the weather than I've ever realized. Good days and sunshine, rain clouds and the blues, they all come and go.

With awareness, I have a choice. I can see these ever-changing patterns as who I am, or I can see them as the feelings of the moment, passing through. When I set myself up for trouble is when I judge myself rather than trust my feelings. Feelings are just feelings; they are not me. I need to remember this, or I will get hooked by judgments and get stuck in the feelings.

Feelings are natural; judging myself for having them is not. To see the rain clouds and sunshine without judgment is freedom. This is all life. I am I, I am a human being, and I am absolutely doing my best, one day at a time, to live happy, joyous and free.

I Will Apply the
Golden Rule to Myself

The voices in my head can get loud. They can whisper, whine, plead and yell at me, all in the same breath. Remembering these voices have no more power over my life than I give them gives me the space I need to choose from my heart.

My voices have been loud lately. For years I have let the chatter in my mind make decisions for me. I believed that chatter was me. Today I know that the chatter is old tapes, old beliefs and feelings, woven together.

When I back off and realize that all my old programming can offer is more of the same, I see how important paying attention to myself is. The keys to reprogramming my way of thinking and interpreting are patience, persistence, compassion and vigilance.

When I don't react to myself, I diffuse my reactions. When I listen to my voices and don't believe them, I undo those old messages. It takes time, and I've got time. I am not using a scorecard; there is no score.

Today I will remember the golden rule, and I will apply it to myself. I will treat myself the way I want others to treat me. Simple, not always easy. No one else has ever been as hard on me as I have been on myself, and no one else can be as good to me as I can be to myself. That is what I will remember today. Taking care of myself will be my pleasure, and I will respect myself. Thank you, Life, for giving me so many chances.

I Had Lots of Secrets

I woke up this morning remembering how imprisoned I used to be by what I thought were my secrets. When my life was in chaos, secrets were the gatekeepers of that insanity. I had lots of secrets. Some of them, I told myself, were protecting others from a truth that would hurt them. Some were protecting me from the reactions of others. Some were just plain lies.

One secret can hold an incredible volume of guilt, fear and shame. Today what I know about my secrets is that the poison they injected into my life, day after day, was far more destructive than the truth ever would have been. My secrets were all lies, one lie serving another lie.

In my journey of recovery, I have realized that the only choice that suits me is the truth, and I do know the truth.

Lies tend to stick in ways that make choosing again very tricky. The truth can change as often as necessary, and in fact, the truth will change with life.

Today I will tell the truth, and I will not intentionally deceive myself or anyone else. Being honest is the doorway to freedom, and freedom is what I want from my recovery.

I Was Just Lost to the World

Step eleven: "Sought through prayer and meditation to improve our conscious contact with the God of our understanding, asking only for knowledge of the Creator's will for us and the power to carry that out." I believe today that deep within there has always been peace. Who we are awaits our return to truth. Through prayer and meditation, truth will be revealed to us.

To live our lives in conscious contact with our Creator is as close as the beat of our hearts. Today I will focus on my heartbeat and listen with all my love to the direction offered there. When I abandoned myself, I abandoned my relationship with the God of my understanding. As I return to myself, I find that grace is there to embrace me as though I had never left.

Maybe the truth is I never really did leave; I was just lost to the world. No more. I am here. Thank you, Creator, for allowing those of us who stray so far the blessing of coming home again.

Who I Am Is Not Something
I Have to Figure Out

I read some astrology info yesterday about my day and time of birth. It was interesting that so much of the information seemed to fit my nature. The profile was like a character snapshot of who I was underneath all the insanity and fear that had become my life.

Then last night I dreamed that I was trapped in a carnival world where everything was distorted, not what it appeared to be. All the people in my dream were also trapped, but they had all forgotten they didn't belong there. They all believed the carnival dreamworld was real.

At the end of the dream, a little person selling tickets to the freak shows looked me straight in the eye and said that if I ever was going to escape this nightmare, I had to let go of my fear of the carnival world and trust who I was. He then laughed and said good luck. In that instant I knew that who I really am is not something I have to figure out. Who I really am is who I was created to be, and all I have to do is have faith enough to be that, without doubts or the need for validation. I had to trust myself.

Recovery has become a much grander event than I first assumed it would be. There is no turning back now. I will never again settle for the world as I used to believe it was. Today I am showing up for myself and am grateful for all the insights and information. This is the real deal. This is the journey toward happy, joyous and free.

She Asked for Suggestions

Last night I watched a friend in an overblown reaction over not getting her way. She had asked for suggestions about her choices in recovery, and when she didn't like the response, she went stupid. I saw me in her. I saw how fear and resistance to change can trap us in insanity.

My friend's reaction went from loud yelling to storming out the door. By the time she left, her own anger and fear had backed her into a corner. No one else was even responding.

It's amazing the power we can give the voices in our heads. What I saw clearly, for the first time, was how the disease of our thinking can separate us from any awareness of the truth. In reaction we not only lose our ability to reason mindfully, we also lose our ability to hear outside our own chaotic internal dialogue. I have been in that same situation a thousand times, and I have only hurt myself.

Witnessing her scene, without reacting myself, was real validation. I'm more grateful for my own awareness of progress than I am interested in her drama. Easy does do it. Progress is perfection. I hope my friend finds what she's looking for.

It works if you work it.

My Beliefs About Myself

Everything in my life is affected by my beliefs about myself. My beliefs about myself are the most important beliefs I hold. The choices I make, the feelings I have, where my faith is invested, my perception of life itself, all are connected to my beliefs about myself.

In recovery I am responsible for my beliefs. Up until I began this journey of recovery, my beliefs were the result of how and what I was taught growing up. From my parents, to grade school, to my peers, television, movies, college and religion, my beliefs were the result of the world around me. All of that is natural. That is the way all animals learn to live in their environment.

In recovery all of that is subject to my willingness to take responsibility for what I believe and for myself. This is my life, and no one but I decides what I will believe as an adult. This is my gateway to freedom. Taking responsibility is the key to that gateway. Addressing my beliefs will be a process in itself. I will need to seek points of view that will support me in questioning my belief system.

Recovery has become about the transformation of who I am. As my beliefs unravel, all of the old stuff that no longer serves me will reveal itself. The choice is mine from that point on. Recovery is my commitment to myself. I will live happy, joyous and free: happy with what I believe about myself, joyous in life and free of all that would go against me. That is what I believe today, and that is the truth.

The Choices Were Great

I am busy. There is a lot going on in my life. Looking at the coming weekend, I realized I had to decide what I really wanted to do because I couldn't do it all. The choices were great. What a transformation! My weekends have moved from insane, self-indulgent binges to being fun and fulfilling. The potential downside has gone from getting busted, or OD'ing, to not being able to do all the good things I have to choose from.

This weekend I'm just going to take it easy. I'm tired. Weekends are a time for rest, and resting sounds wonderful. I am so grateful to have friends and family I can just hang out with. I am comfortable being myself today. I don't have the need to get high to sit still. I'm not paranoid about what the people I'm with think about me.

If I get uncomfortable, I'll go to a meeting. Seeing how far my life has come is all the motivation I need to keep taking care of myself. Gratitude is so sweet. I really had no idea that life could be like this. Thank you, Me. Easy does it in action.

It Was a Total Assumption

I am not a yoga kind of guy. At least that's what I believed. This morning I woke up, and my body felt so good. There was no tension, no laziness. I felt like my whole being had been stretched out, and it felt amazing. Yesterday I participated in my first yoga class. I thought I didn't like yoga. There I go, thinking again. What I thought about yoga was not from experience; it was a total assumption. When I got into it I loved it. Once again my life has connected with something my mind had written off.

I am really learning the meaning behind the saying, "Don't believe yourself." If I had believed my thinking, I would not have gone to the yoga class.

By keeping my attention on how I feel rather than on what I think, I'm finding a whole new level of awareness and freedom.

Recovery is about living outside the box I am recovering from. That covers a lot of life. What I will remember is: I need to question my opinions, always; assumptions are dumb; this is my life—it's up to me to live it; and taking care of my body feels great.

Last but not least, when it comes to yoga class, I will keep coming back.

For Me, God Is Life

I hear all kinds of conversations and opinions about God, and who cares? I'm a human being; I don't believe being human includes an understanding of God. Does a little fish understand the ocean? I don't need anyone to agree with my feelings or thoughts about a Creator. What I trust today is that the greatest offering I can give to whatever my interpretation of God is, is the way I live my life.

If God created me then taking care of myself is the highest form of offering back to the Creator. I am life. The Creator creates life. I can't separate the Creator from the creation. One is an extension of the other. I am here to live life, and today I am taking responsibility for my life.

All I see resulting from the need to define or interpret God is self-indulgent arrogance, anger, hate and war. I don't believe, whatever God is, that any creator of life would appreciate our self-righteous destruction of that creation. Whether we're talking about one country attacking another, or one individual harming him- or herself, none of that is a reflection of love or appreciation for life.

Today I am grateful for my life. I am grateful for my recovery and the freedom that recovery offers. I have made my amends to my Creator for all the ways that I hurt myself, and I have also made a promise that I will do my best to live my life with gratitude, love, loyalty and justice, beginning with myself and continuing with my brothers and sisters—one day at a time.

A Conversation I Really Didn't Care About

I caught myself last night getting involved in a conversation with a group of people over religion. There were all kinds of opinions and attitudes. There was every level of commitment to whatever their personal beliefs were, from agnostic to fundamentalist.

When I realized that I was hooked into a conversation that I really didn't care about I stopped talking and just listened. It is amazing how invested we get in our opinions, and in challenging the opinions of others, when it makes no difference, other than to our egos, what anyone else thinks of our beliefs or what we think of theirs.

For years I have fed into situations that were pointless. I don't want to do that anymore. I want to put my energy and attention into doing what I enjoy. The life I live is the result of where I choose to invest my attention and energy. That is my responsibility. In recovery I will be conscious of the focus of my attention.

If I am not in awareness in the present moment it is easy to slip into old patterns. I feel like I am waking up from a long, foggy coma. So, for today my attention will be on awareness and gratitude. I will love this new way of living in the world, and I will, without judgment, be responsible with my attention.

_____

_____

_____

_____

_____

_____

_____

_____

_____

_____

_____

_____

_____

_____

_____

_____

_____

_____

_____

_____

_____

_____

Our Truth Is Not of This World

Step twelve: "Having had a spiritual awakening as the result of these steps, we tried to carry this message to those who suffer, and to practice these principles in all our affairs." The twelve steps have provided millions of people a refuge from their insanity. Humans are creatures of habit, and habit is a pathway to addiction. With awareness, addiction is only the result of our lost authenticity. Our truth is not of this world.

Our truth is born with us and abandoned by us. By willingness to take action we hold the power to undo all that would go against our relationship with our Creator. When we help others we make our transformation real. The best way of helping others, of sharing the message of recovery, is by taking care of ourselves.

When we live from our truth, our presence affects the lives of everyone we touch. We are not recovering something outside of ourselves; we are recovering who we really are, and that is the work of the angels.

Love is life in action. Walk with your prayers, keep showing up, and remember, don't believe everything you think.

Staying Home Was a Metaphor

Yesterday I stayed home all day. I can't remember the last time I did that, unless I was sick or hungover. My home is my home. You would think I would have an animated, alive relationship with the space I call home, but I really haven't had. For so long my attention was focused on my misery that home became a container for all that suffering.

Since I got into recovery, I have been working so diligently on it that I have not considered my relationship with this space. Yesterday, something inside me said it was time to stop and just be at home. I listen to those voices of the heart these days. It was wonderful. I rearranged some furniture and cleaned out old stuff that I'm no longer attached to. I washed my car and rearranged the cabinets.

Looking back on yesterday I see how staying home was a metaphor for my new relationship with myself. There are many spaces and relationships in my life that will be tended to and rearranged as my process of recovery unfolds.

I used to be afraid of changes; now they excite me. I am no longer so resistant to life. This is living life on life's terms. This is the power of choice giving me back the power of choice. Thank you, Life, thank you.

The Void Is Still There

For many years I lived my life in relationship with the hole in my heart. Loneliness and fear seemed to well up from a void within. That emptiness was all too real. In my addiction, using separated me from the terror of the void. Today the void is still there.

The difference is that today I can be lonely or scared and not have to react to my fear. My addiction developed from a pattern of reaction. I used drugs and alcohol, and most anything else, to medicate my discomfort with myself. Looking within myself for truth I realize that the hole in my heart has begun to heal. Being willing to see myself as a whole person is the revelation that serves that transformation.

Taking responsibility for my reactions allows me the power to choose from integrity rather than from fear. Today I will appreciate myself for the willingness to stay present even when I don't like what I see.

Most of the suffering in my life seems directly related to what I believe. To change beliefs requires staying present, to question those beliefs. It works if you work it, and I am going to work it.

By My Own Hand I Have Suffered

Life is not personal. I have, for lack of knowing better, taken life very personally. By my own hand I have suffered. To take an inventory of myself I have to begin with the structure that I've come to identify as me. Perceptions of myself are all filtered through beliefs about myself. When I clean up my relationship with myself I change my perception of everything around me.

This work has to come from the inside out if it is going to resolve confusion and clarify relationships. Clarity is my goal today. Recovering me is really uncovering me, one day at a time.

The Balance of Spirit and Form

Earth, air, fire and water are the elements of creation. When touched by the spirit of life, form awakens to consciousness.

Our bodies are of the earth. Our bodies have an awareness of their own. Listen!

Our emotions are of water. They flow through and around our lives. Feel!

Our minds are of the air. Like the vapors of thought and concept they are seemingly real, yet formless until action is taken. Be aware!

Fire is the spirit of life. Fueled by the source of creation, transforming thought, emotion and form into the action of our being.

Happy, joyous and free comes as the balance of spirit and form. Being in recovery is being the caretaker of all the elements of our constitution.

Today I live with awareness of the parts that make me whole, embracing each as a gift to be nurtured and explored. Today I will be in gratitude to all those aspects of my being, mindful that the harmony of mind, body and spirit is the foundation that recovery is built upon.

Changes Happened Anyway

All I really own in life is experience. Houses, cars, people, money, they all come and go. I may believe something today and not believe the same thing tomorrow. This world is in a state of continuous evolution. Recovery is realigning myself with the flow of life.

I spent years resisting change. Changes happened anyway. I believed for a long time that accomplishment led to security and safety. I accomplished a great deal and still was not happy. The answer to being happy in life seems to be simply to enjoy being alive.

Now that is a tall order! To be happy just being alive takes all the power out of expectation and fear. When you love being alive, misery becomes a choice. My addictions are miserable experiences, and for today I choose to love this life and let go of the temptation to suffer.

The Truth About the Wants

There is a great temptation that lurks in the recesses of my mind. This temptation has been my companion since I was a child. I am certain that I was predisposed to develop this condition, and develop it I did. The affliction I am talking about is the wants. The wants are not a clinically acknowledged malady; yet this condition can be potentially harmful to health and well-being.

Primary symptoms are disproportionate desires in relation to actual needs. A secondary symptom is a brat-like reaction to not feeding the wants.

There is one proven, absolute antidote for this plague. That is gratitude. To be grateful for our lives instantly puts the wants in proper perspective. Gratitude offers all the fulfillment and joy we seek from the insanity of the wants.

The bottom line is if you are grateful for life itself, then you will see the truth, and the wants will lose their power over you.

About the Author

An apprentice of the nagual Don Miguel Ruiz, Lee McCormick is founder of The Ranch, a holistic recovery treatment center located on two thousand acres in Tennessee, and Spirit Recovery, Inc. He is currently the program consultant at Renaissance Malibu, a world-class healing and treatment facility, where he implements the spirit recovery model at their facility in Malibu, California. He shares his time between the Santa Monica Mountains above Malibu and his ranches in Tennessee.

For more information on Spirit Recovery treatment programs visit *www.recoveryranch.com* or call The Ranch at 800-849-5969.

Visit *www.spiritrecovery.com* for information on journeys, workshops, conferences and training.